Children's Authors

Shel Silverstein

Cari Meister
ABDO Publishing Company

visit us at
www.abdopub.com

Published by ABDO Publishing Company, 4940 Viking Drive, Suite 622, Edina, Minnesota 55435. Copyright © 2001 by Abdo Consulting Group, Inc., P.O. Box 398166, Minneapolis, Minnesota 55439 USA. International copyrights reserved in all countries. No part of this book may be reproduced in any form without written permission from the publisher.

Published 2001
Printed in the United States of America
Second Printing 2002

Photos: AP/Wideworld (pages 5, 17, 19, 21), Corbis (pages 7, 9, 13, 15), Timepix (page 11)
Editors: Bob Italia, Tamara L. Britton, Kate A. Furlong, Christine Fournier
Art Direction: Neil Klinepier

Library of Congress Cataloging-in-Publication Data

Meister, Cari.
    Shel Silverstein / Cari Meister.
        p. cm. -- (Children's authors. Set 2.)
    Includes index.
    ISBN 1-57765-483-8
        1. Silverstein, Shel--Juvenile literature. 2. Authors, American--20th century--Biography--Juvenile literature. 3. Children's stories--Authorship--Juvenile literature. [1. Silverstein, Shel. 2. Authors, American.] I. Title. II. Series.

PS3569.I47224 Z79 2001
818'.5409--dc21
[B]

00-049602

Contents

Shel Silverstein

Shel Silverstein is one of America's most loved children's authors. His poems and drawings have captured the imagination of children for nearly 40 years.

As a child, Shel spent time learning to write and draw. He got his first job as a cartoonist at an army newspaper. After leaving the army, he started to write cartoons for magazines.

One of Shel's friends convinced him to write for children. At first, Shel refused. But then he changed his mind. His first children's book was *Uncle Shelby's Story of Lafcadio, the Lion Who Shot Back*.

Shel's first book was successful. He continued to write more children's books. He also wrote music. And he wrote some plays.

Shel Silverstein died in 1999. But his humor and original children's poems will be read by fans for many years to come.

Shel Silverstein

Learning to Draw

Sheldon Allan Silverstein was born in Chicago, Illinois, on September 25, 1930. His parents were Helen and Nathan Silverstein. He had a sister named Peggy. The Silversteins lived in a Chicago neighborhood called Logan Square.

Young Shel liked baseball. He dreamed of becoming a baseball player one day. But Shel was not good at baseball. He couldn't throw or catch a ball well.

So Shel began to spend his time writing and drawing. He had never read the works of famous writers. So he had no one to imitate or **admire**. This allowed him to create his own special style.

Logan Square, Chicago

School Days

Shel attended Roosevelt High School. He also worked at Comiskey Park, where the Chicago White Sox play baseball. For four years, he sold hot dogs to the fans.

After high school, Shel attended college. First, he went to the University of Illinois at Navy Pier. He studied art. But he left after a year. Then he attended the Chicago Academy of Fine Arts for a year.

Next, Shel went to Roosevelt University. There, he studied English for three years. He also worked on the school's newspaper, *The Torch*.

Shel liked working on the newspaper. But he disliked his college classes. He wanted to see the world.

Roosevelt University

Military Man

*I*n 1953, Shel was **drafted**. The U.S. needed men to serve in the **Korean War**. So Shel left college to become a soldier in the army. At first, he served in Korea. Then he was sent to Tokyo, Japan.

As a soldier, Shel worked for *The Stars and Stripes*. It was a newspaper for people serving in the army. Shel worked for the Pacific edition of the newspaper, called *Pacific Stars and Stripes*. Shel drew daily cartoons for the paper. It was his first real job as a cartoonist.

Shel's cartoons were **satires** of army life. Sometimes he made fun of sergeants. This got him in trouble. Shel drew cartoons for the *Pacific Stars and Stripes* until he left the army in 1955.

Two men reading **The Stars and Stripes**

Getting Started

After leaving the army, Shel looked for work. He had a hard time finding a job as a cartoonist. But after a year, Shel was finally able to sell his cartoons to a magazine.

People liked Shel's cartoons. They wanted him to write books. From 1960 to 1963, Shel wrote three humorous books. The books had cartoons in them.

Shel's good friend, Tomi Ungerer, liked the books. Ungerer wrote children's books. He thought Shel would be good at writing children's books. But Shel did not think so.

Ungerer convinced Shel to talk with an **editor**. He arranged a meeting between Shel and Ursula Nordstrom. Nordstrom worked at a large **publishing house** called Harper.

Nordstrom wanted Shel to write a children's book for Harper. Shel finally agreed. So in 1963, he wrote *Uncle Shelby's Story of Lafcadio, the Lion Who Shot Back*. Children and grown-ups enjoyed Shel's book.

Opposite page: Two children enjoy reading Tomi Ungerer's Zeralda's Ogre.

Books & Music

Shel's next book was *The Giving Tree*. He asked an **editor** named William Cole to publish it. Cole worked at a **publishing house** called Simon & Schuster. Cole rejected *The Giving Tree*. He said people would not buy it.

But Harper agreed to publish *The Giving Tree* in 1964. Many people bought the book. It made Shel famous.

Shel also published three other children's books in 1964. These books were *Uncle Shelby's Giraffe and a Half*, *Uncle Shelby's Zoo: Don't Bump the Glump*, and *Who Wants a Cheap Rhinoceros?*

Then Shel took a break from children's books. He started writing music. From 1968 to 1971, he wrote the **scores** for several movies. They included *Ned Kelly* and *Who Is Harry Kellerman and Why Is He Saying Those Terrible Things about Me?*

Shel also wrote many folk songs. He worked on albums with other musicians. Shel wrote a song called "A Boy Named Sue." It became a hit for country singer Johnny Cash. In 1969, both Shel and Cash won **Grammy Awards** for the song.

While Shel worked on his music, he became a father. He and a woman named Susan Hastings had a daughter in 1970. They named her Shoshanna. They called her Shanna for short.

Johnny Cash

More Books

Shel returned to writing children's books in 1974. That year he wrote *Where the Sidewalk Ends*. It was filled with Shel's poems and line drawings. They showed the world in a fresh and surprising way, which many readers enjoyed.

In 1976, Shel wrote *The Missing Piece*. It was about a circle that is missing a wedge-shaped piece. The circle rolls along looking for its missing piece. Shel then wrote a **sequel** to this book, called *The Missing Piece Meets the Big O*.

Shel spent a lot of time writing and drawing books for children. But he also had time to work on other projects. He worked on another book for grown-ups in 1979. A year later, he recorded a country music album. It was called *The Great Conch Train Robbery*.

Opposite page: Shel was nominated for an Academy Award in 1990 for his song "I'm Checkin' Out" from the movie **Postcards from the Edge.**

Poetry & Plays

*I*n 1981, Shel wrote a book of humorous poems and drawings for children. It was called *A Light in the Attic*. He **dedicated** it to his daughter Shanna. Sadly, Shanna died the next year.

Soon, Shel began to write plays. His first play was put on in New York in 1981. It is a one-act play called *The Lady or the Tiger Show*. Shel based it on a short story by Frank Stockton.

In 1984, Shel once again became a father. His son was named Matthew. During this time, Shel wrote several more full-length plays. He worked on a collection of one-act plays. And he won another **Grammy Award** for a recording of *Where the Sidewalk Ends*.

In 1988, he co-wrote a **screenplay** with the famous **playwright** David Mamet. Their film was called *Things Change*.

In 1996, Shel wrote his last book, *Falling Up*. It is another collection of poems and drawings for children. Shel did not write any more children's books before he died on May 10, 1999.

A Light in the Attic

poems and drawings by

Shel Silverstein

Shel Silverstein's Fame

Shel's children's books have been popular with children and adults for many years. *A Light in the Attic* was on the *New York Times* best-seller list for more than three years. This is rare for any children's book. It is even more rare for a book of children's poetry.

Shel's children's books have also won awards. *Where the Sidewalk Ends* was named a *New York Times* Notable Book in 1974. It also won the Michigan Young Readers Award in 1981. That same year, *School Library Journal* named *A Light in the Attic* a Best Book. In 1982, *The Missing Piece Meets the Big O* won the Children's Choice Award from the International Reading Association.

Shel's poems and drawings have delighted children for nearly 40 years. Many of his books are still best-sellers among young and old alike. Though Shel is gone, his work lives on.

Opposite page: Shel Silverstein won awards for both music and writing during his career.

21

Glossary

admire - to think of with respect or approval.

dedicate - to inscribe a book to a friend or family member to show respect.

draft - to be selected for military service. People who are drafted must serve in the armed forces.

editor - a person who makes sure a piece of writing has no errors in it before it is published.

Grammy Award - an award given each year for the best musicians and recordings.

Korean War - a war between North Korea and South Korea that lasted from 1950 to 1953. The American government sent troops to help South Korea.

playwright - a person who writes plays.

publishing house - a business that produces and offers printed materials for sale to the public.

satire - writing that makes fun of qualities of human life.

score - music written to accompany a play or movie.

screenplay - the script for a movie.

sequel - a book or movie that continues a story begun in a
   previous one.

Internet Sites

http://www.harperchildrens.com
Click on MEET THE AUTHOR, scroll down to Search and type
in Silverstein. Read about the author, and click on the book
covers to learn more about his books.

**http://www.harperchildrens.com/hch/author/features/
silverstein.asp**
A tribute to Shel Silverstein from Harper Collins Children's
Books. Learn more about Shel's career, and read one of his
poems.

*These sites are subject to change. Go to your favorite search engine and
type in Shel Silverstein for more sites.*

Index